7/08

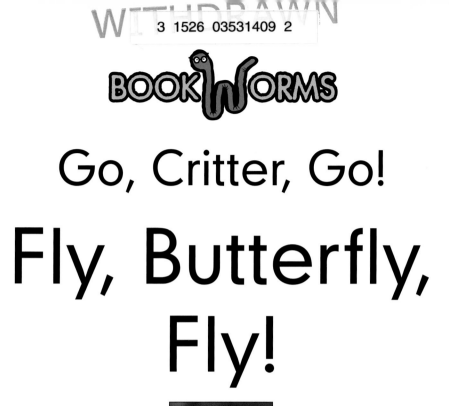

BOOK WORMS

Go, Critter, Go!

Fly, Butterfly, Fly!

Dana Meachen Rau

Marshall Cavendish
Benchmark
New York

Butterflies have four wings.

3

Butterflies have six legs.

Butterflies have lots of colors.

Butterflies start as caterpillars.

Caterpillars turn into butterflies.

Butterflies sit on flowers.

Butterflies drink from flowers.

Butterflies fly.

Fly, butterfly, fly!

Words We Know

caterpillar

colors

drink

flowers

fly

legs

wings

Index

Page numbers in **boldface** are illustrations.

About the Author

Dana Meachen Rau is an author, editor, and illustrator. A graduate of Trinity College in Hartford, Connecticut, she has written more than one hundred fifty books for children, including nonfiction, biographies, early readers, and historical fiction. She lives with her family in Burlington, Connecticut.

With thanks to the Reading Consultants:

Nanci Vargus, Ed.D., is an Assistant Professor of Elementary Education at the University of Indianapolis.

Beth Walker Gambro received her M.S. Ed. Reading from the University of St. Francis, Joliet, Illinois.

Marshall Cavendish Benchmark
99 White Plains Road
Tarrytown, New York 10591-9001
www.marshallcavendish.us

Library of Congress Cataloging-in-Publication Data

Rau, Dana Meachen, 1971–
Fly, butterfly, fly! / by Dana Meachen Rau.
p. cm. — (Bookworms. Go, critter, go!)
Summary: "Describes characteristics and behaviors of butterflies"—Provided by publisher.
Includes index.
ISBN-13: 978-0-7614-2649-3
1. Butterflies—Juvenile literature. I. Title. II. Series.
QL544.2.R385 2007
595.78'9—dc22
2006034226

Editor: Christina Gardeski
Publisher: Michelle Bisson
Designer: Virginia Pope
Art Director: Anahid Hamparian

Photo Research by Anne Burns Images

Cover Photo by *Animals Animals*/Stephen Dalton

The photographs in this book are used with permission and through the courtesy of:
Corbis: pp. 1, 19 Fritz Rauschenback/zefa; pp. 3, 21BR Laura Sivell/Papilio; pp. 13, 20BR Darrell Gulin;
pp. 17, 21T James L. Amos. *Animals Animals*: pp. 5, 7, 20TR, 21BL Fabio Medeiros Columbini;
pp. 9, 11, 20TL Patti Murray; pp. 15, 20BL Arthur Evans.

Printed in Malaysia
1 3 5 6 4 2